W9-BWB-975

Date: 4/13/17

J BIO ASHE
Strand, Jennifer,
Arthur Ashe /

Arthur Ashe

Jennifer Strand

abdopublishing.com

Published by Abdo Zoom™, PO Box 398166, Minneapolis, Minnesota 55439. Copyright © 2017 by Abdo Consulting Group, Inc. International copyrights reserved in all countries. No part of this book may be reproduced in any form without written permission from the publisher. Abdo Zoom™ is a trademark and logo of Abdo Consulting Group, Inc.

Printed in the United States of America, North Mankato, Minnesota
072016
092016

Cover Photo: Harry Harris/AP Images
Interior Photos: Harry Harris/AP Images, 1, 7; AP Images, 4, 9, 12, 14, 15, 19; Dave Pickoff/AP Images, 5, 10–11; iStockphoto, 6; Marty Lederhandler/AP Images, 11; Gerry Cranham/The LIFE Images Collection/Getty Images, 13; Mike Lien/New York Times Co./Getty Images, 16–17; Bettmann/Getty Images, 18

Editor: Brienna Rossiter
Series Designer: Madeline Berger
Art Direction: Dorothy Toth

Publisher's Cataloging-in-Publication Data
Names: Strand, Jennifer, author.
Title: Arthur Ashe / by Jennifer Strand.
Description: Minneapolis, MN : Abdo Zoom, [2017] | Series: Trailblazing athletes
    | Includes bibliographical references and index.
Identifiers: LCCN 2016941530 | ISBN 9781680792485 (lib. bdg.) |
    ISBN 9781680794168 (ebook) | 9781680795059 (Read-to-me ebook)
Subjects: LCSH: Ashe, Arthur--Juvenile literature. | Tennis players--United
    States--Biography--Juvenile literature. | African American tennis players--
    Biography--Juvenile literature.
Classification: DDC 796.342092 [B]--dc23
LC record available at http://lccn.loc.gov/2016941530

Table of Contents

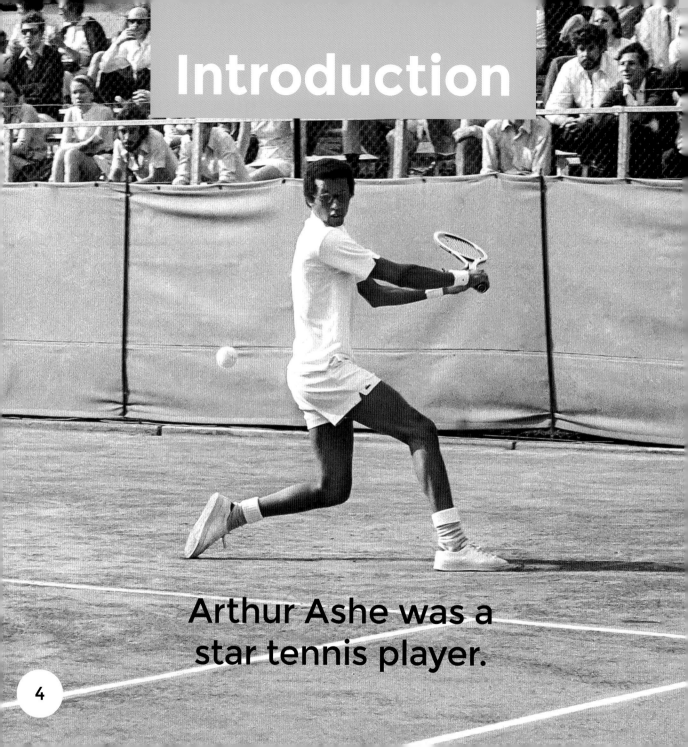

Introduction

Arthur Ashe was a
star tennis player.

He was also an **activist**.
He helped people be treated fairly.

Early Life

Arthur was born on July 10, 1943.
He grew up in Virginia.

He started playing tennis
when he was six years old.

The United States was **segregated**. Most tennis players were white. Many would not play against Arthur.

But he kept playing.
He worked hard.

Leader

Ashe became one of the world's best players. He won the US Open in 1968.

No black man had won it before.

Ashe later went to South Africa. Black people there faced **discrimination**, too.

Ashe tried to
help them.

In 1975 Ashe won Wimbledon.

It is one of the most important tennis events. He was the first black man to win it.

Legacy

Ashe worked for civil rights. He was calm. He was polite. Many people liked him.

This helped him change unfair rules.

Ashe used his fame to help others.
He trained young **athletes**.

He was a teacher, too.
On February 6, 1993, he died.

Arthur Ashe

Born: July 10, 1943

Birthplace: Richmond, Virginia

Sport: Tennis

Known For: Ashe was a civil rights activist and tennis player. He was the first black man to win the Australian Open, the US Open, and Wimbledon.

Died: February 6, 1993

1943: Arthur Robert Ashe Jr. is born on July 10.

1968: Ashe wins the US Open.

1969: Ashe helps start a group to protect tennis players' rights. The group becomes the Association of Tennis Professionals in 1972.

1975: Ashe wins Wimbledon.

1988: Ashe publishes *A Hard Road to Glory*. It is about the history of black US athletes.

1993: Ashe dies on February 6.

Glossary

activist - a person who works for change.

athlete - a person who plays a sport.

civil rights - the rights of all citizens to be treated equally and fairly.

discrimination - when a group of people is treated unfairly.

segregated - keeping one group of people separate from others, often in a way that is unfair.

Booklinks

For more information
on **Arthur Ashe**, please visit
booklinks.abdopublishing.com

Z⌕m™ In on Biographies!

Learn even more with the Abdo Zoom
Biographies database. Check out
abdozoom.com for more information.

Index